MW01154316

A Journal for Recording the Surprising Things Children Say

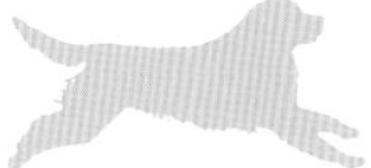

Published by Boston Mills Press, 2008
132 Main Street, Erin, Ontario N0B 1T0
Tel: 519-833-2407 Fax: 519-833-2195

In Canada:
Distributed by Firefly Books Ltd.
66 Leek Crescent
Richmond Hill, Ontario, Canada L4B 1H1

In the United States:
Distributed by Firefly Books (U.S.) Inc.
P.O. Box 1338, Ellicott Station
Buffalo, New York 14205

The publisher gratefully acknowledges for the financial support of our publishing program
the Canada Council, the Ontario Arts Council, and the Government of Canada
through the Book Publishing Industry Development Program (BPIDP).

Design by Gillian Stead
Printed in China

Oh, What You Said!

This is something we always mean to do,
want to do, plan to do . . .

. . . write down the memorable things
that we hear our children say.

Try as we might to remember them later – we often don't.

Here is your chance to record that funny or moving,
enlightened or profound, wise or whimsical statement.

A record to share with your children
when they are all grown up.

Here is your chance to never forget.

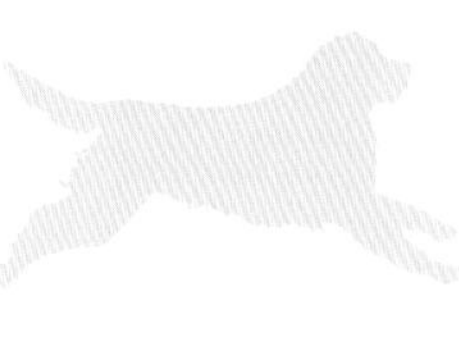

Photo
Here

“

”

Details

"

"

Details

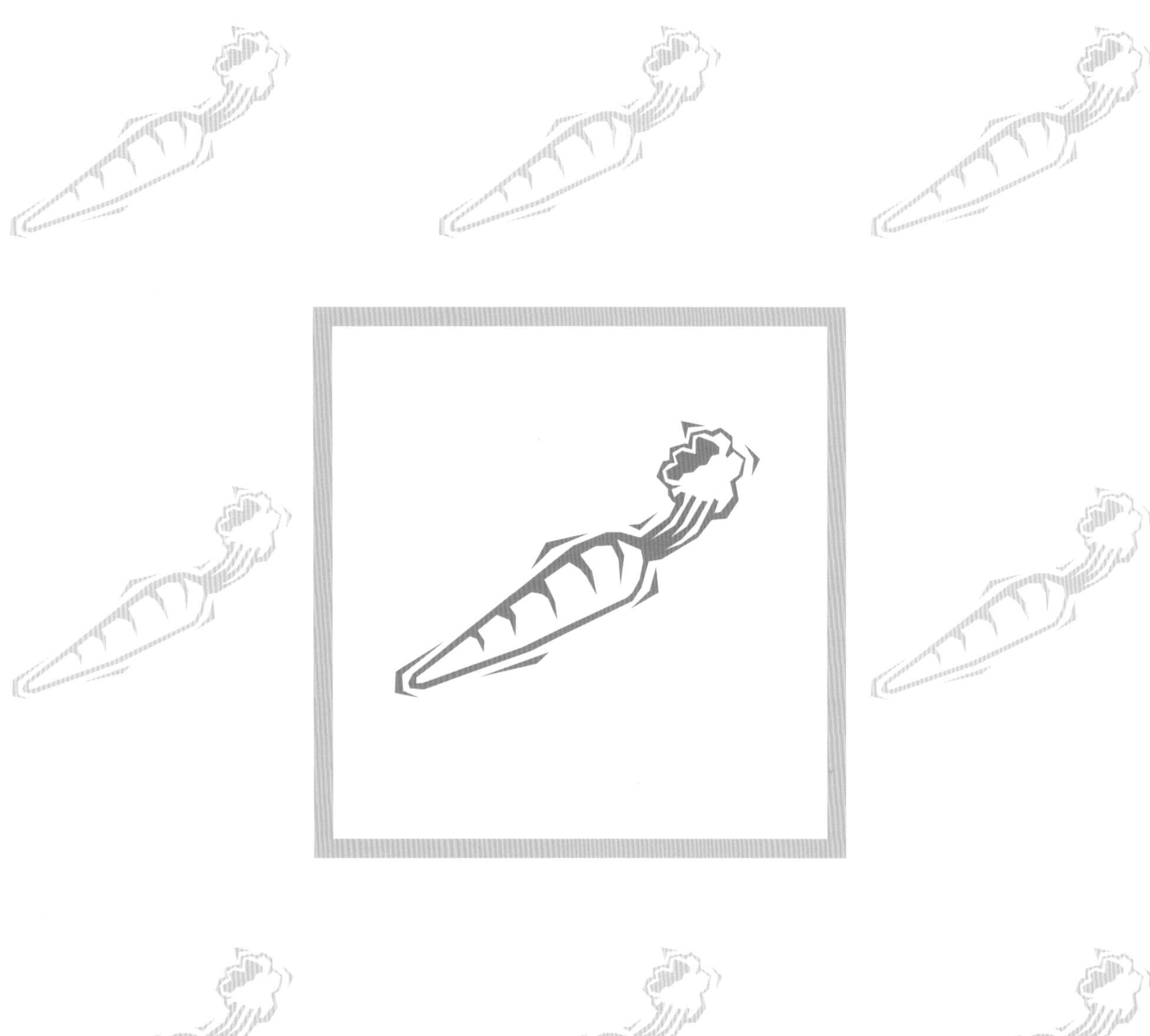

“

”

Details

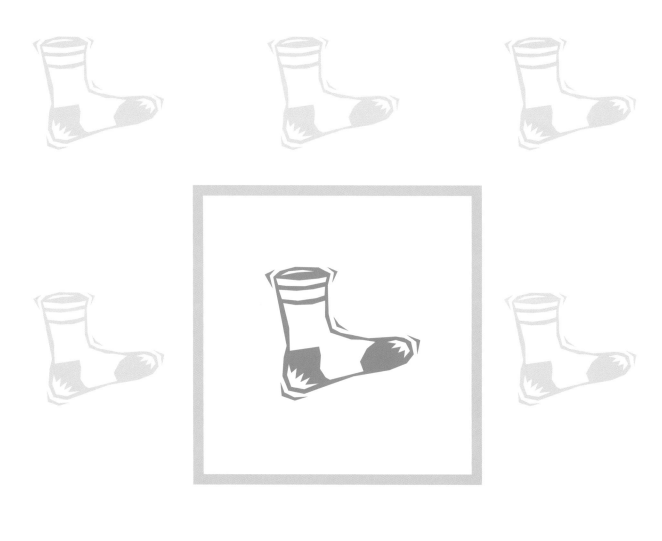

“

”

Details

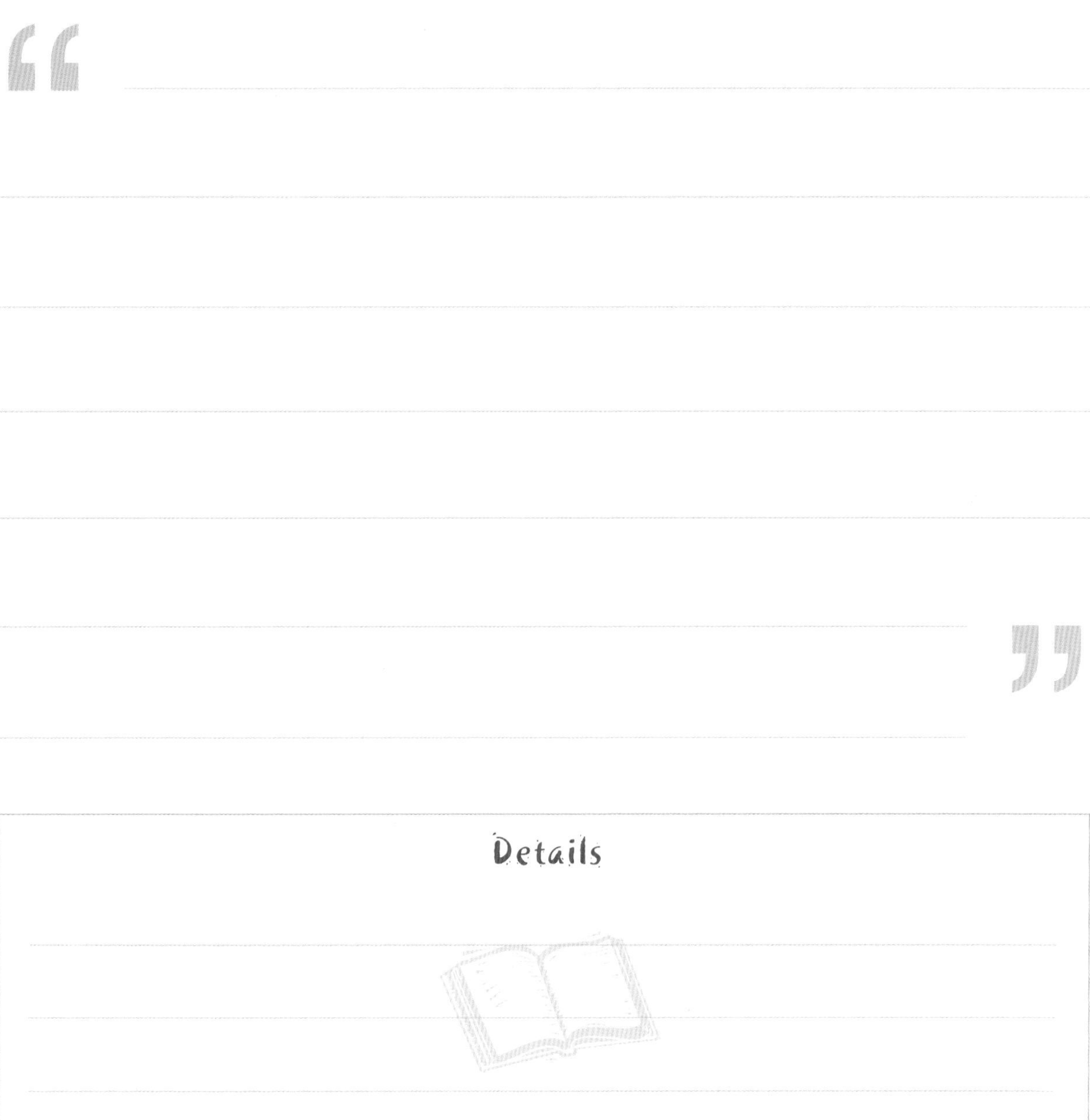

Details

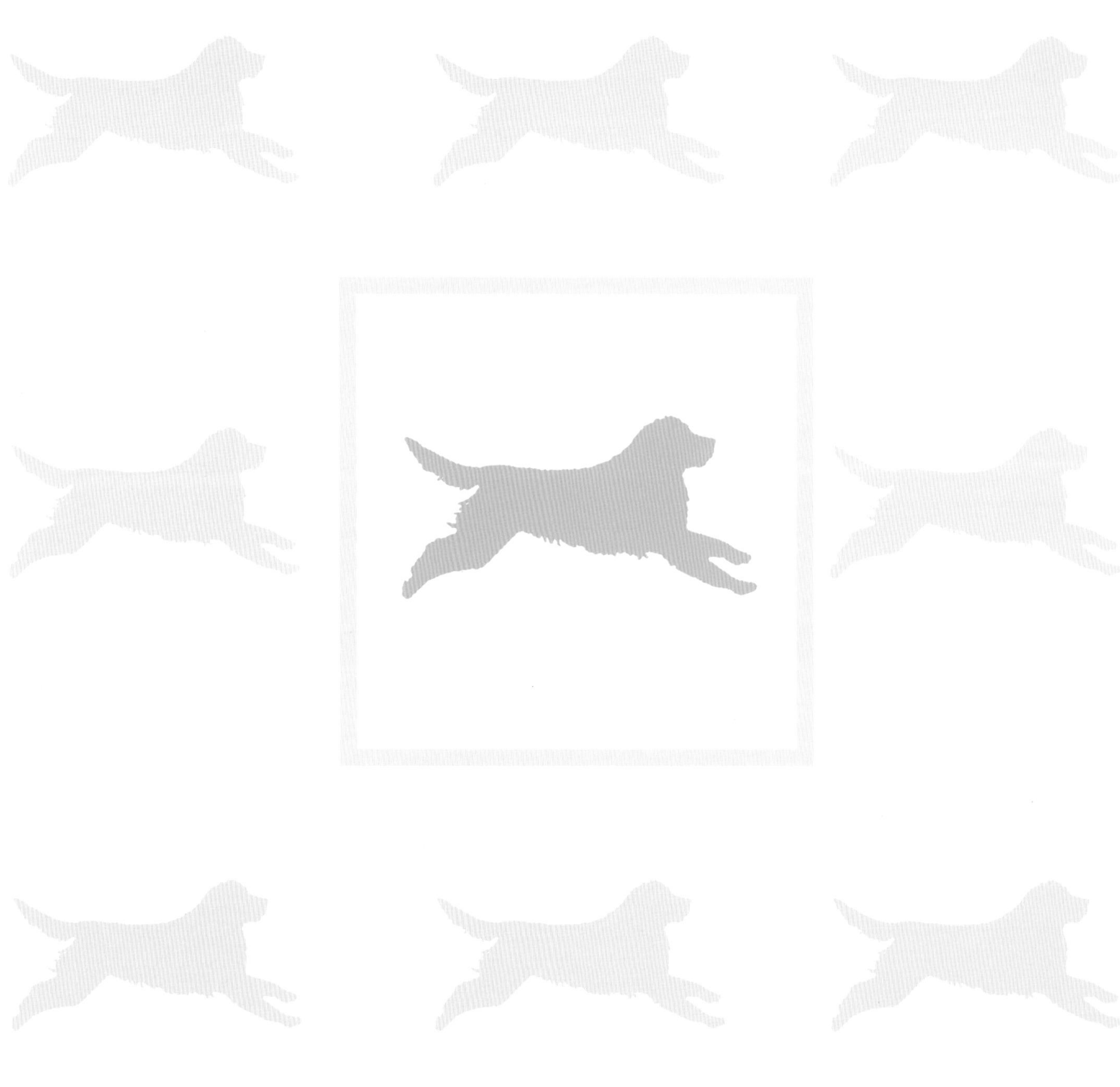

“

”

Details

“

”

Details

" "

Details

“

”

Details

Details

“

”

Details

“

”

Details

""

Details

Details

""

Details

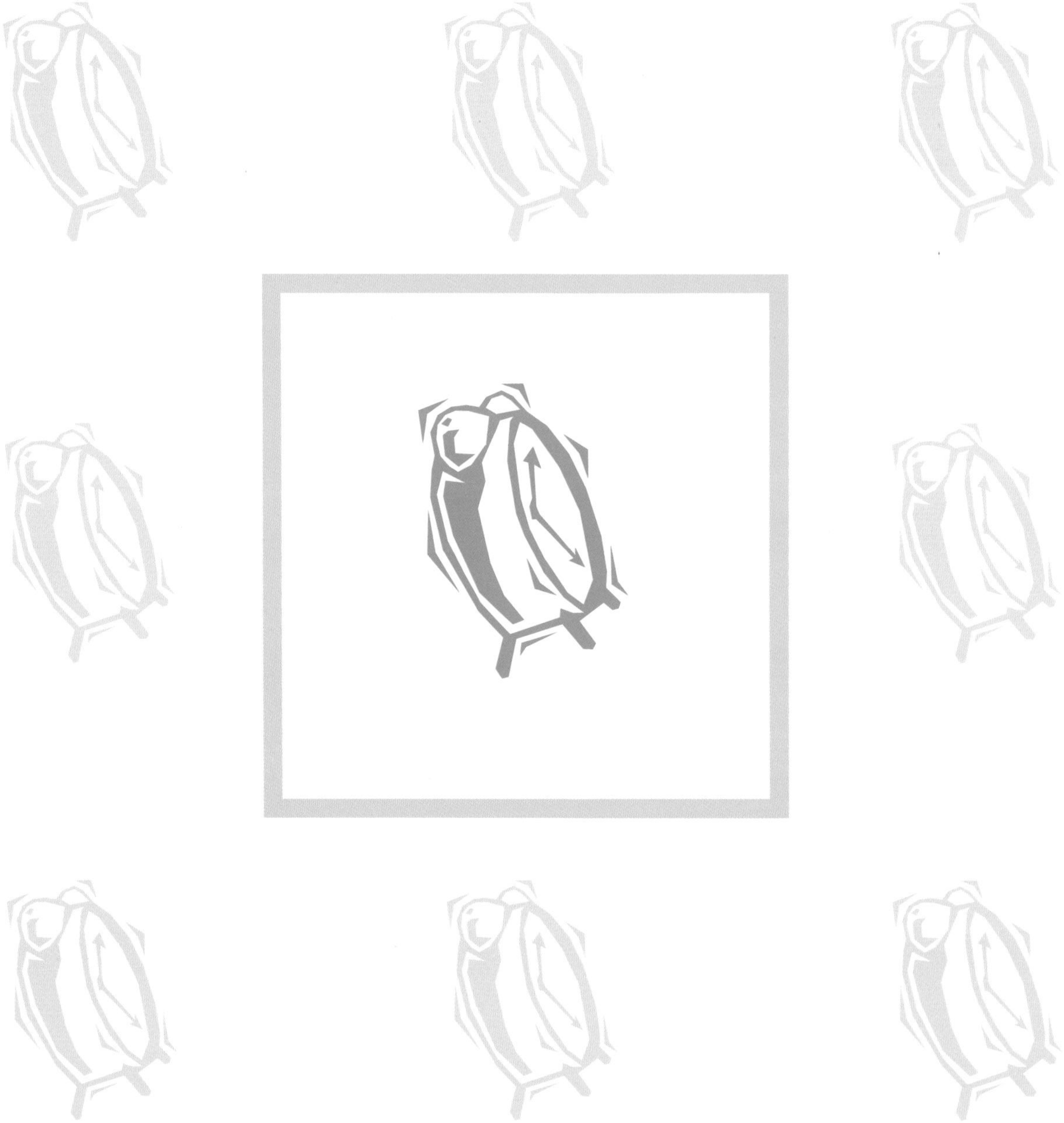

Details

“

”

Details

Details

“

”

Details

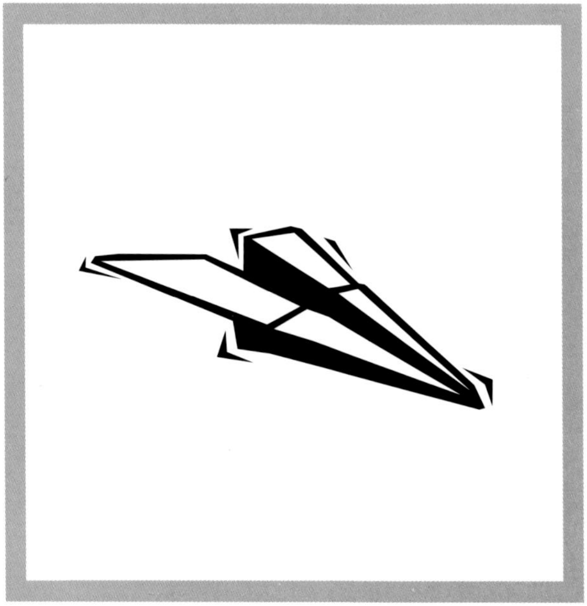

“

”

Details

“

”

Details

“

”

Details

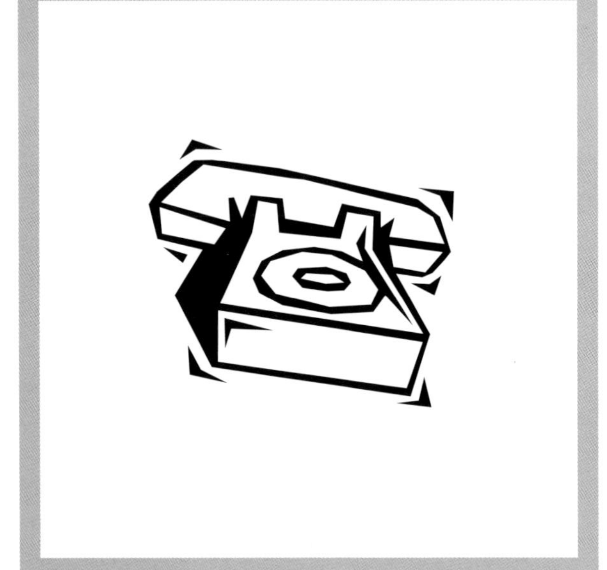

“

”

Details

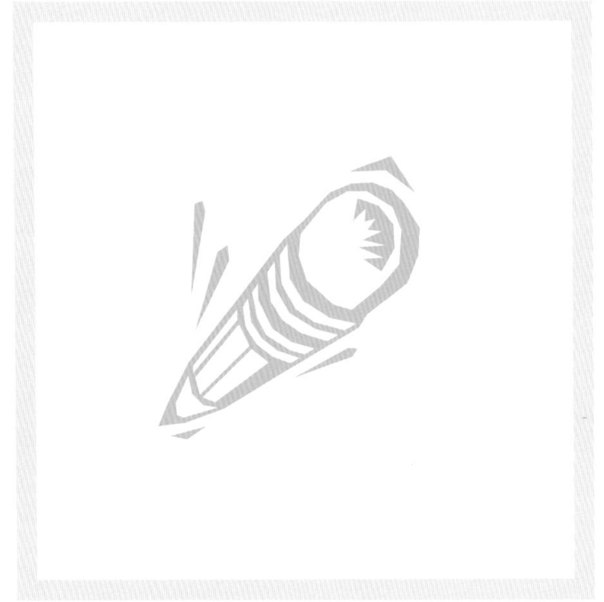

“

”

Details

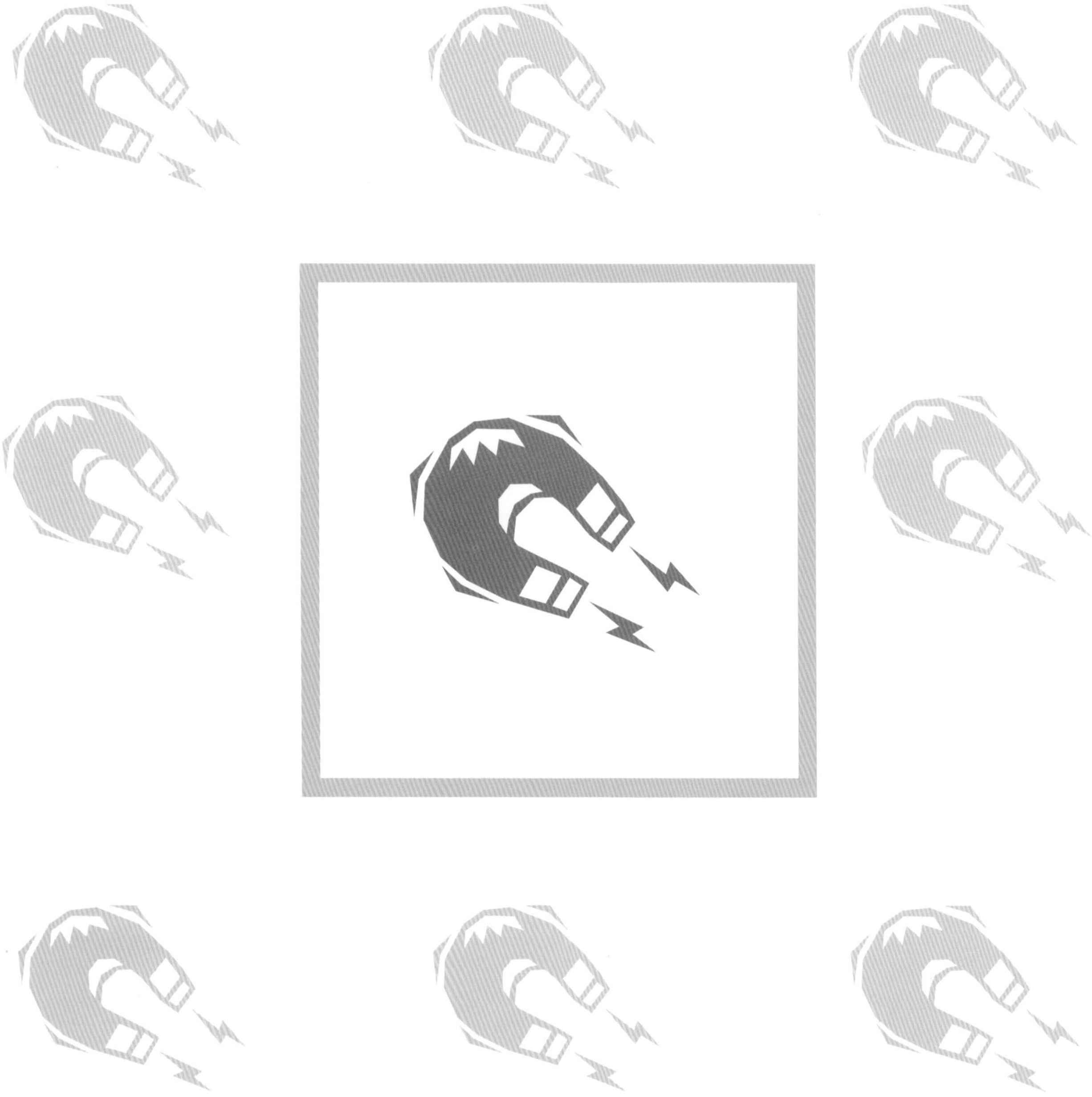

Details

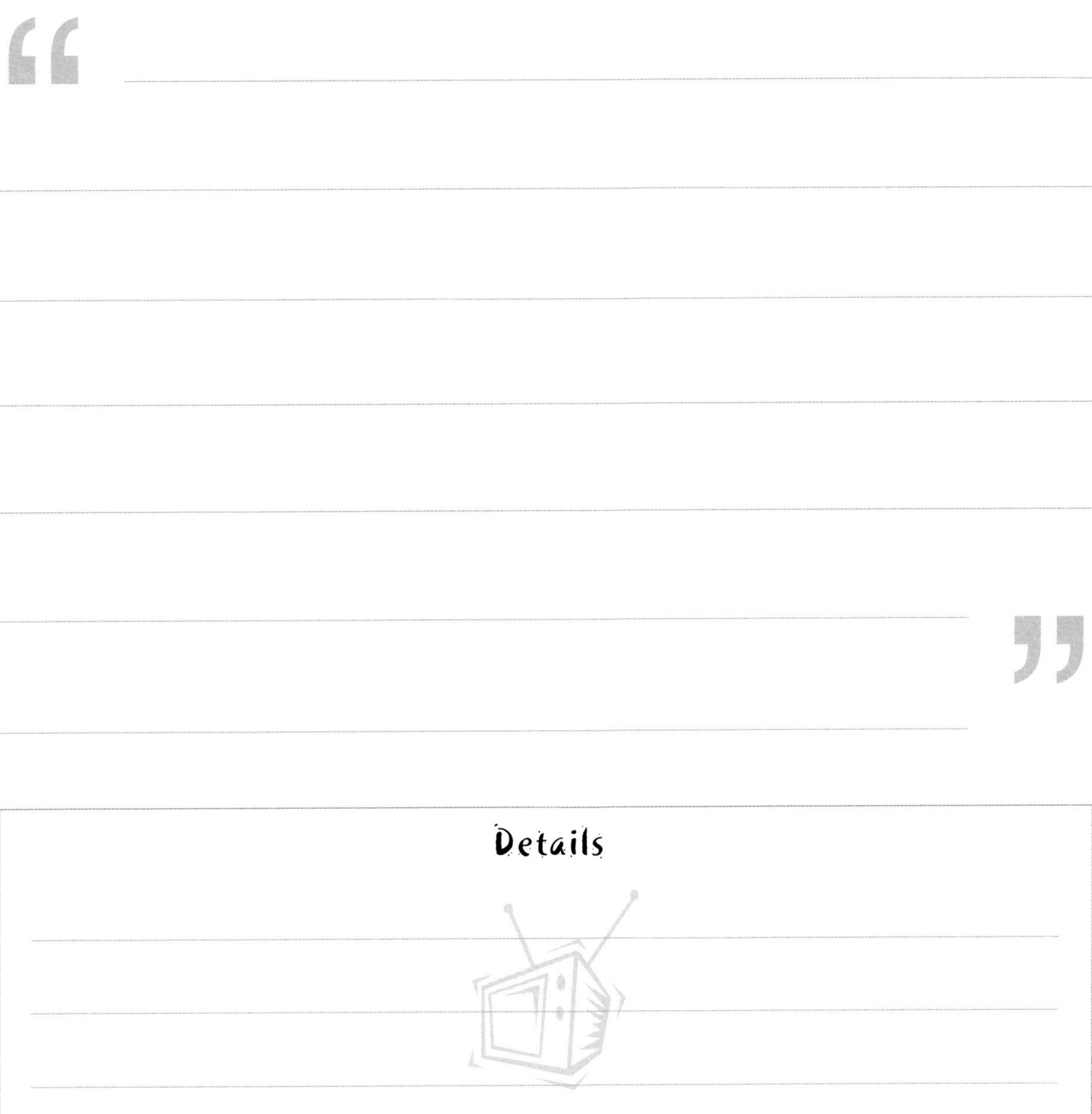
Details

"

"

Details

Details

“

”

Details

Photo
Here

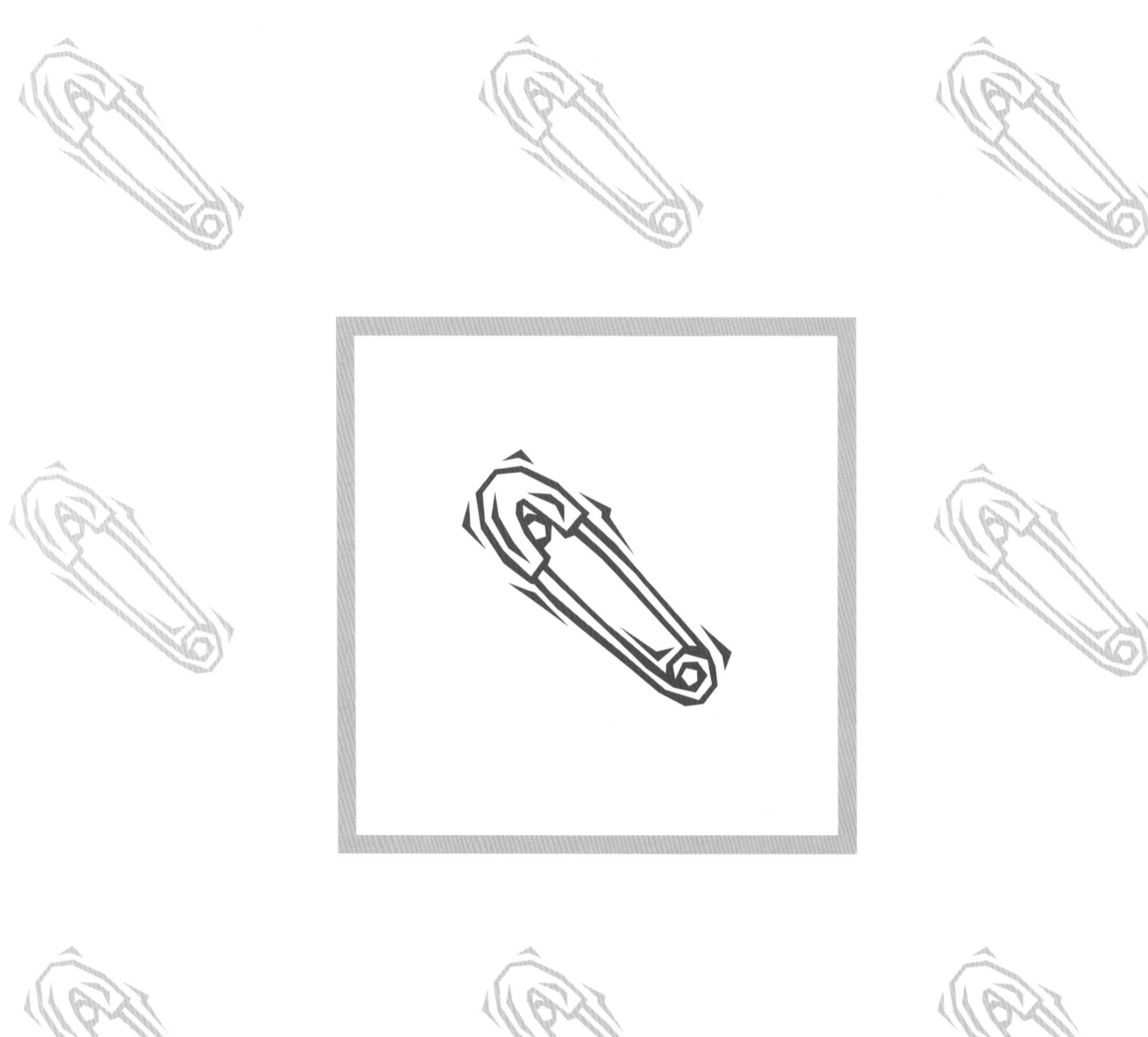

""

Details

“

”

Details

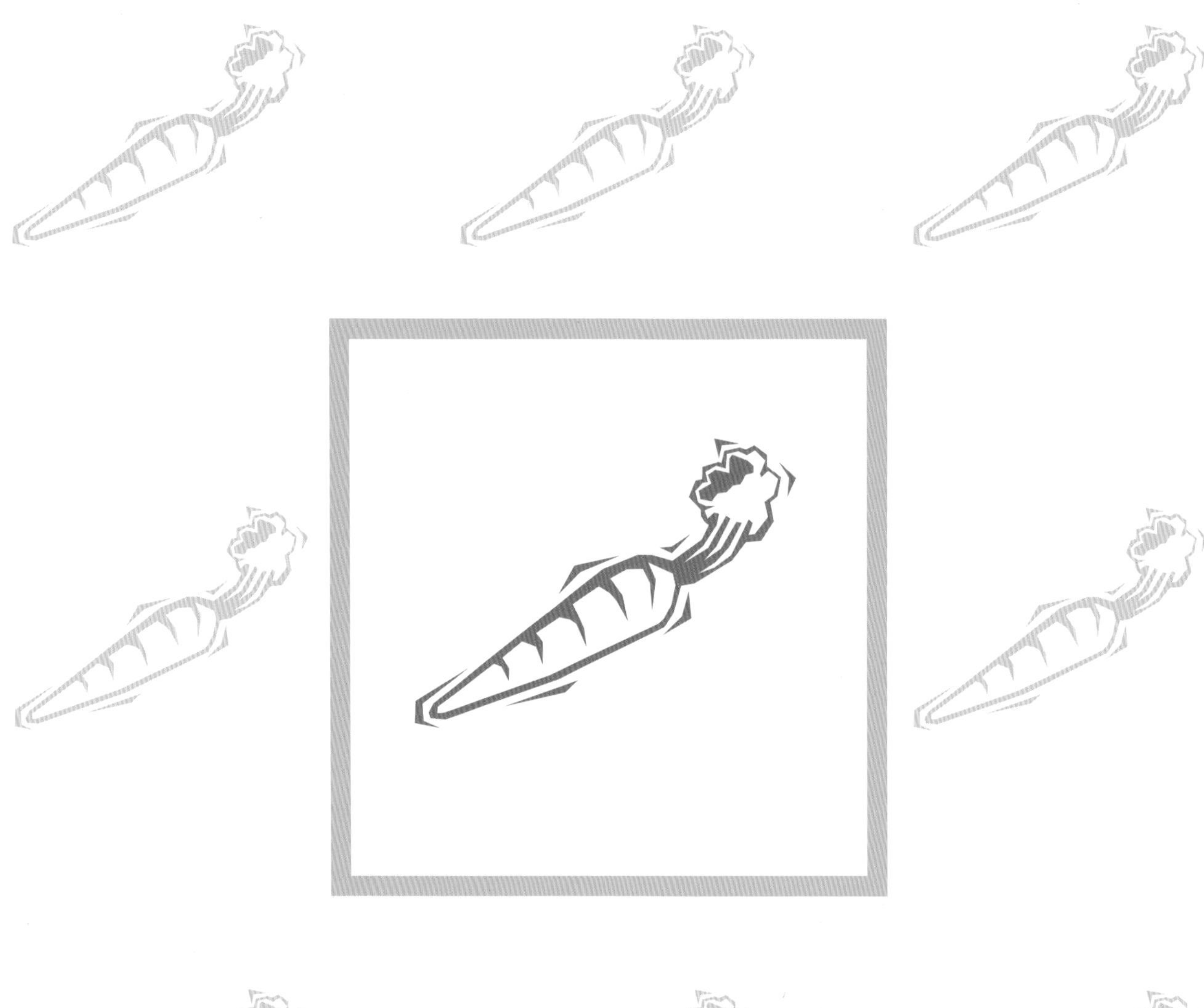

""

Details

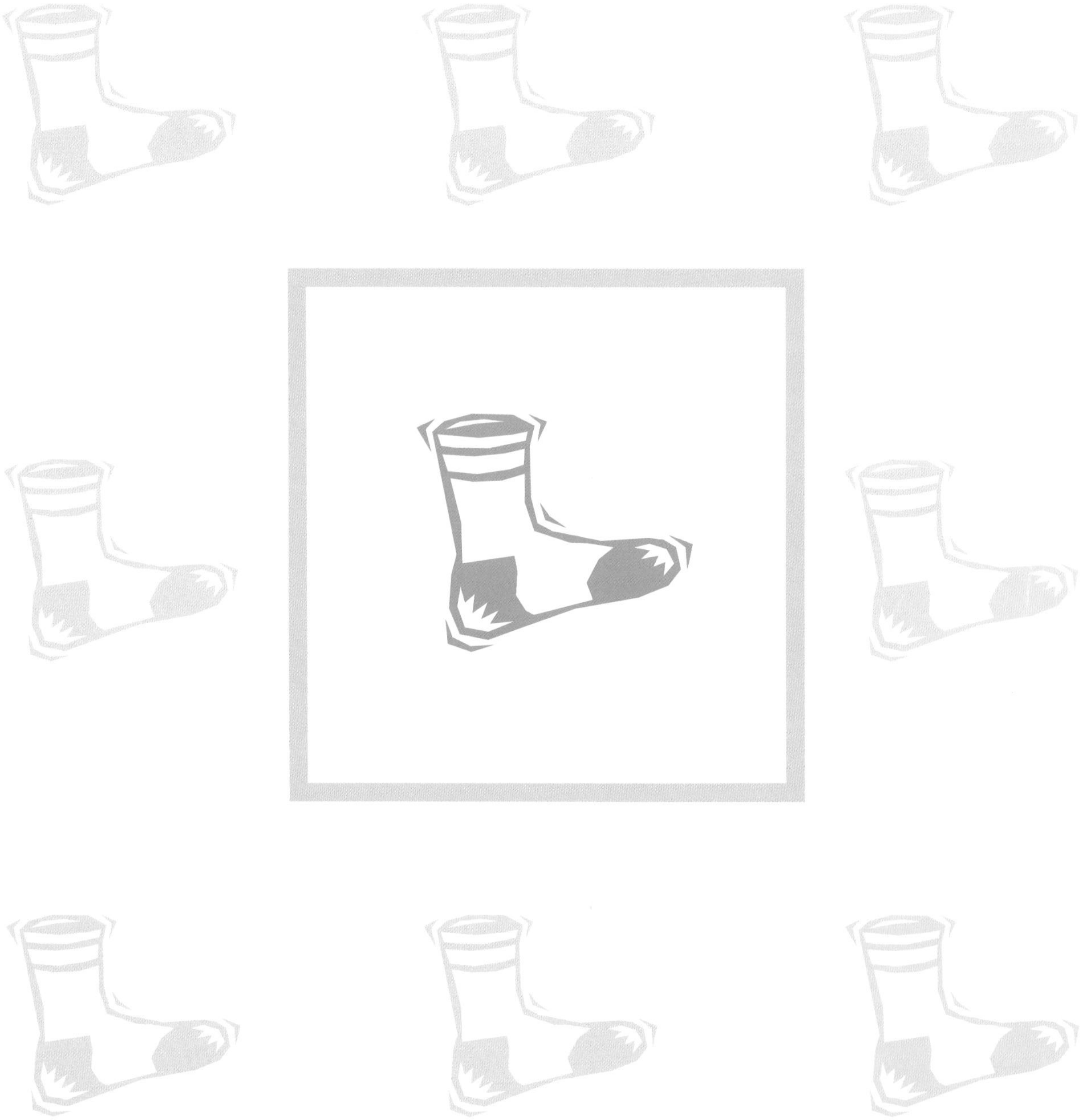

“

”

Details

“

”

Details

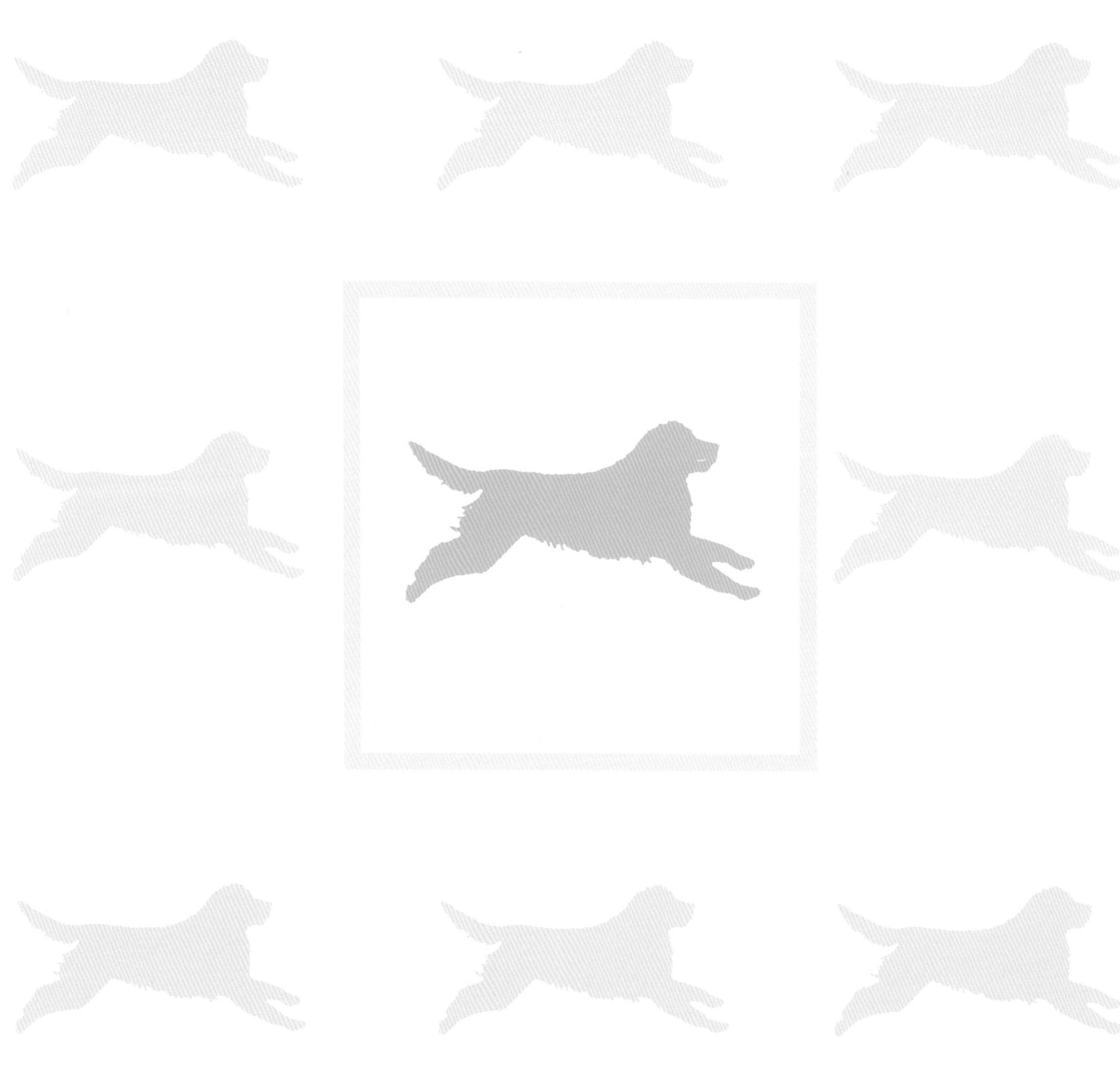

“

”

Details

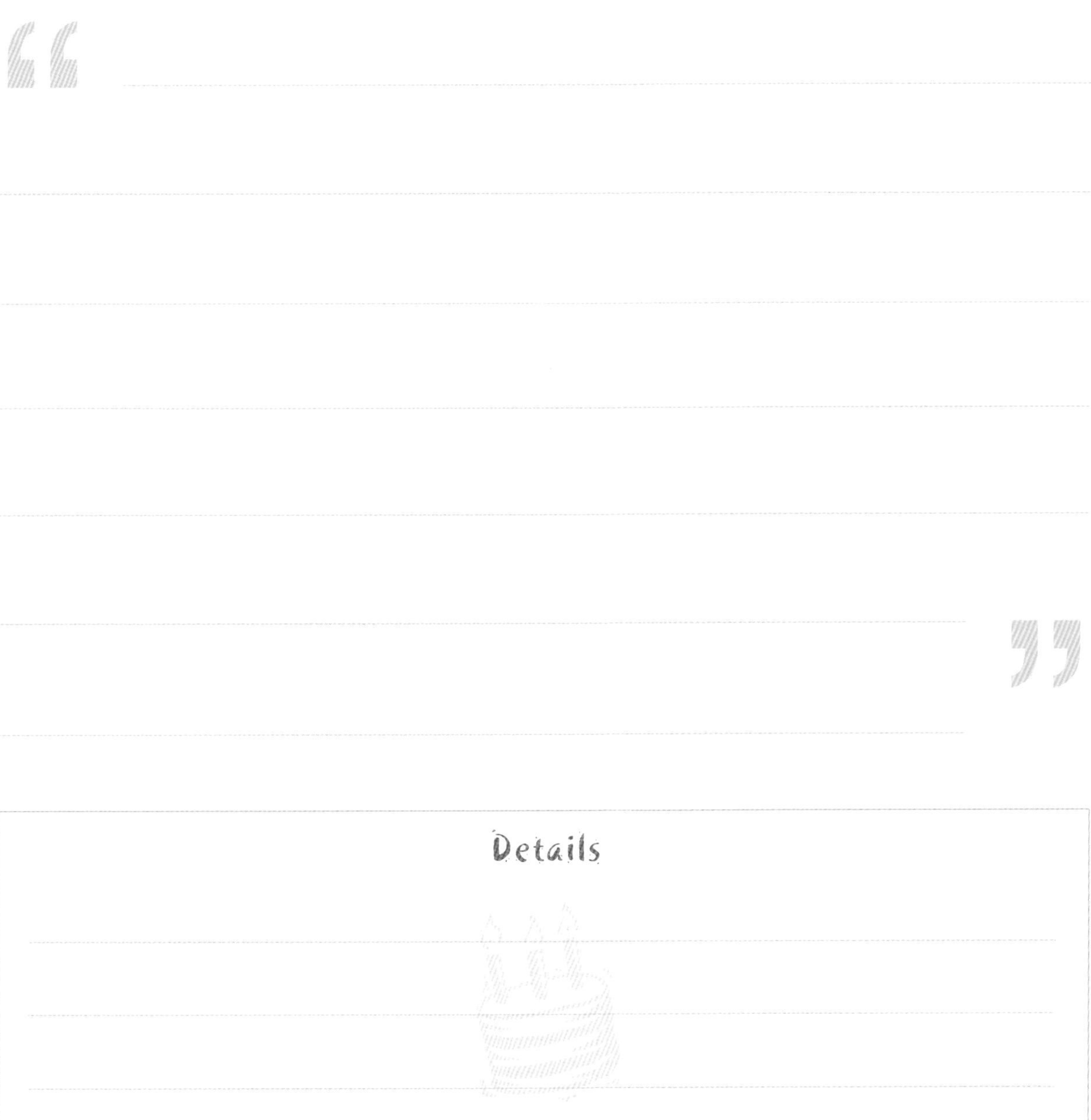

Details

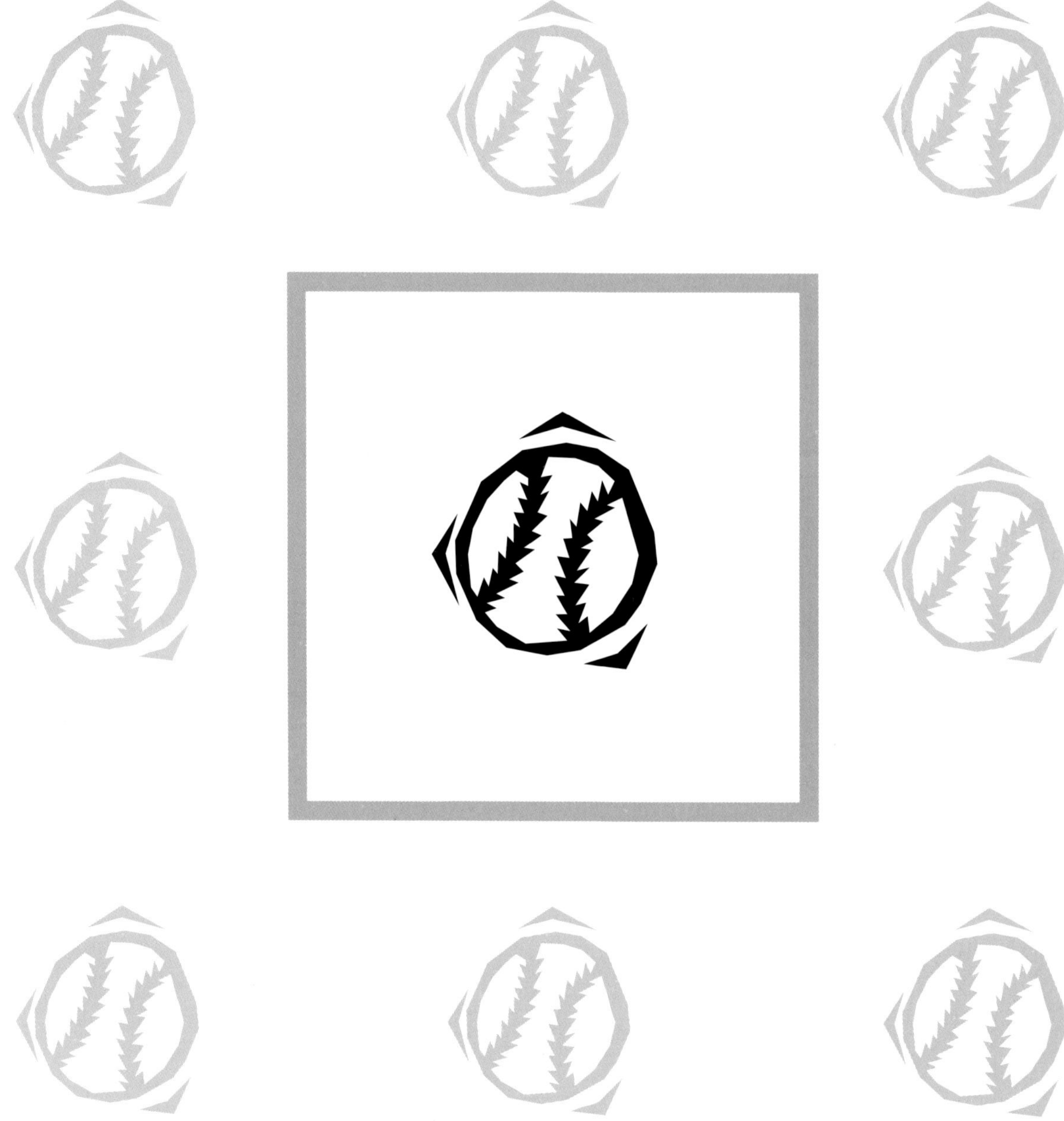

“

”

Details

“

”

Details

Details

“

”

Details

Details

“

”

Details

“

”

Details

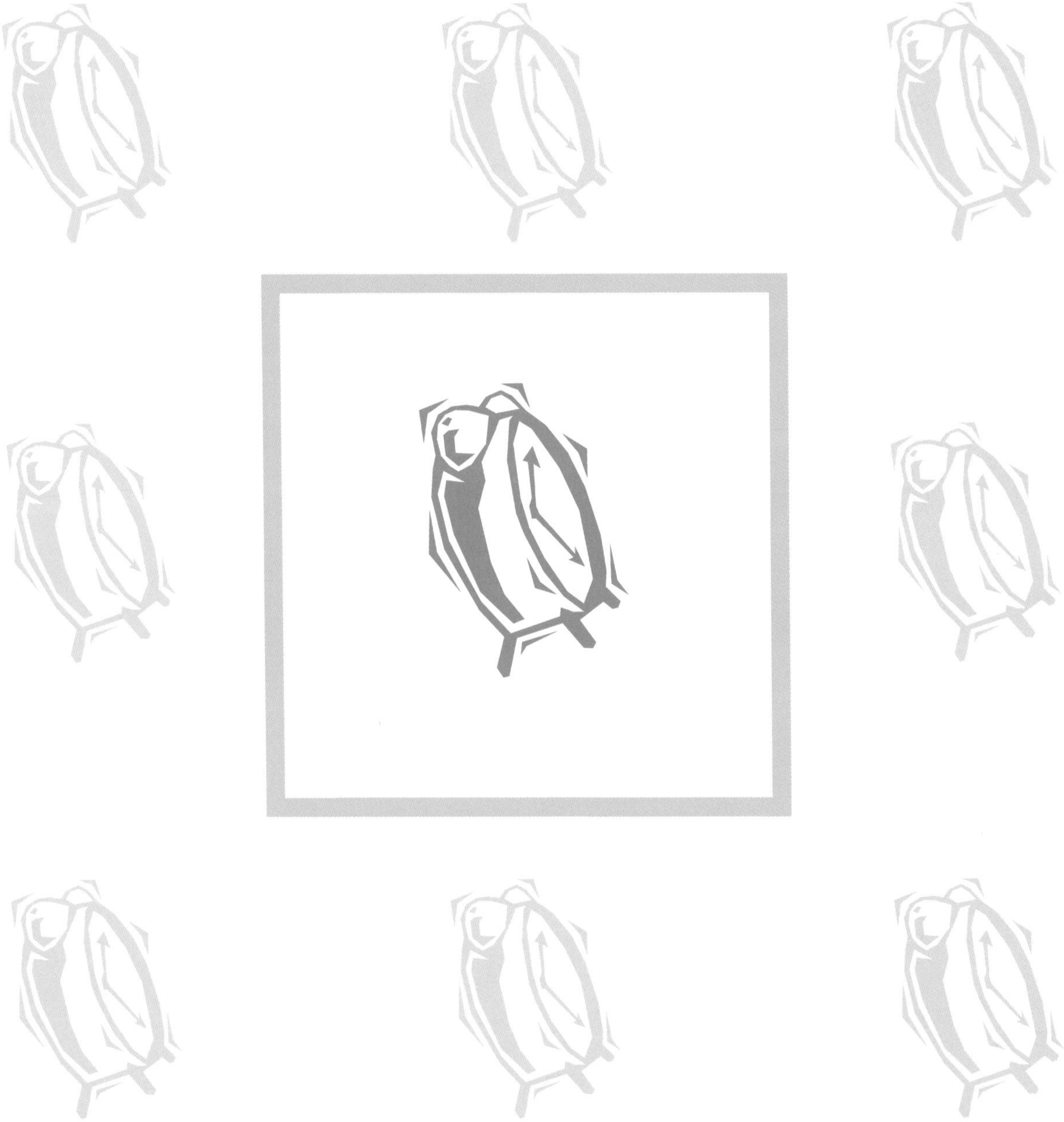

“

”

Details

Details

""

Details

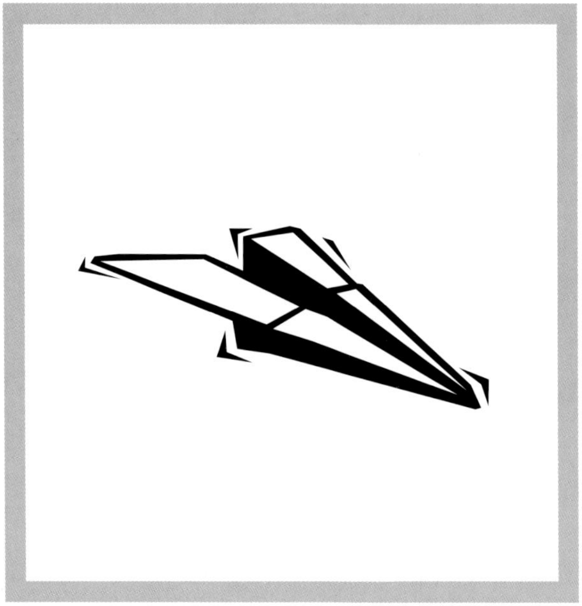

“

”

Details

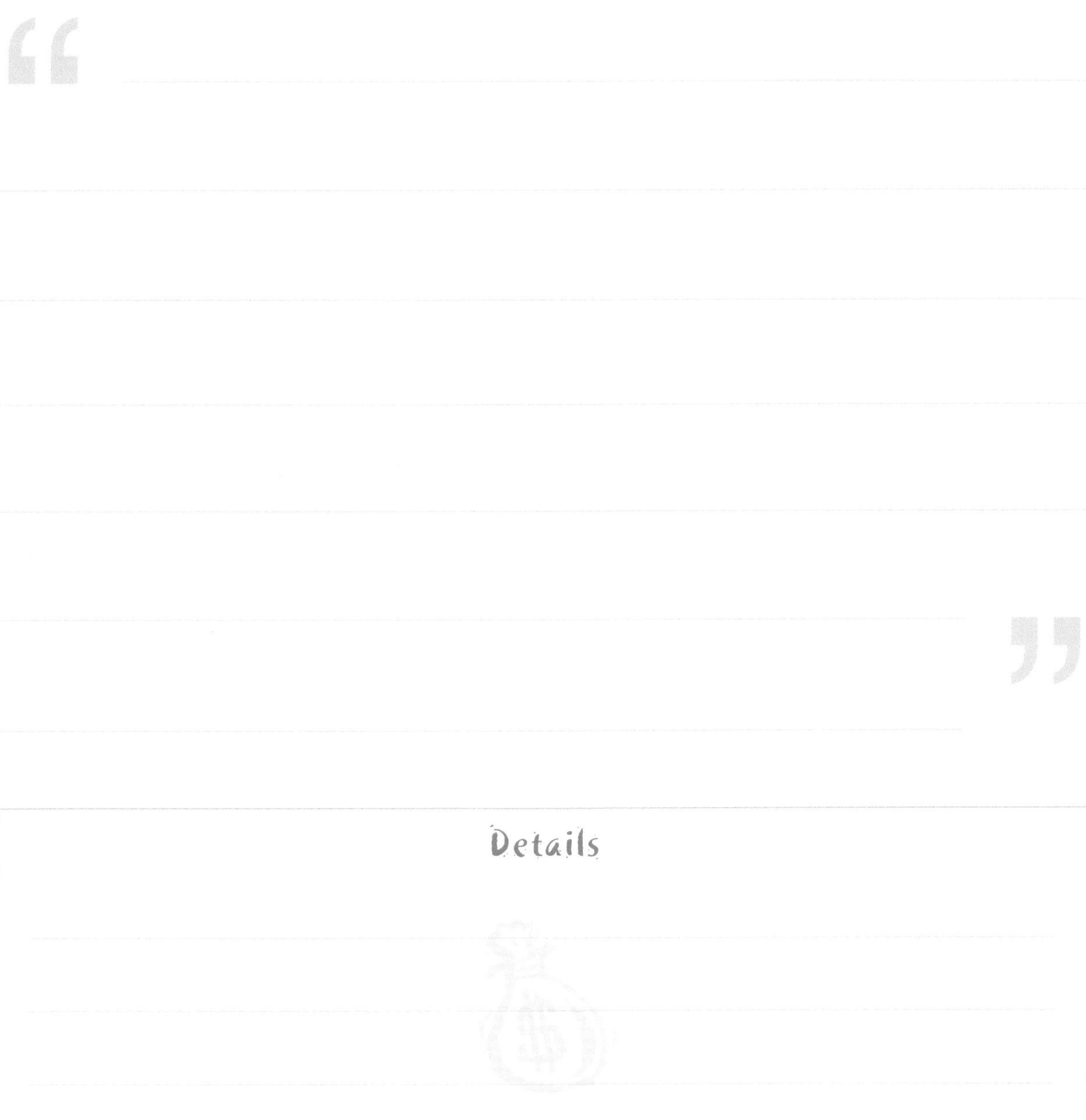

Details

“

”

Details

“

”

Details

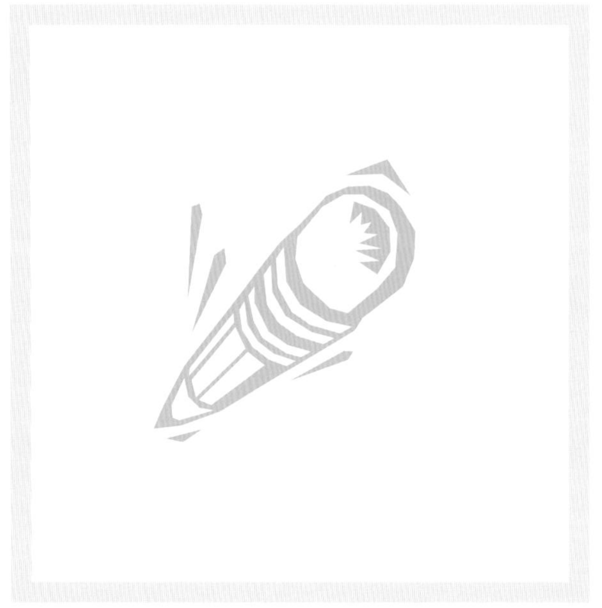

“

”

Details

“

”

Details

Details

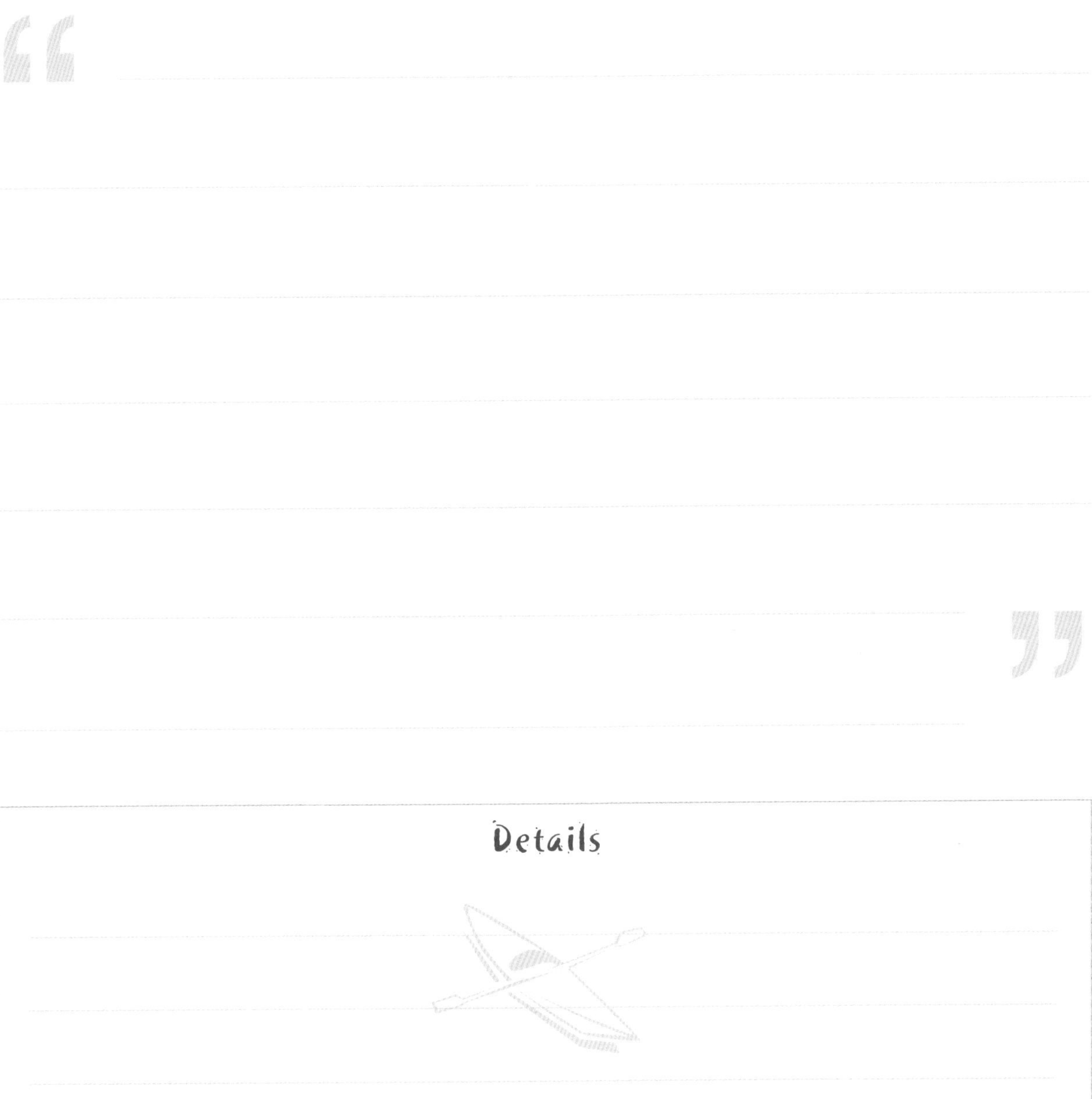

Details

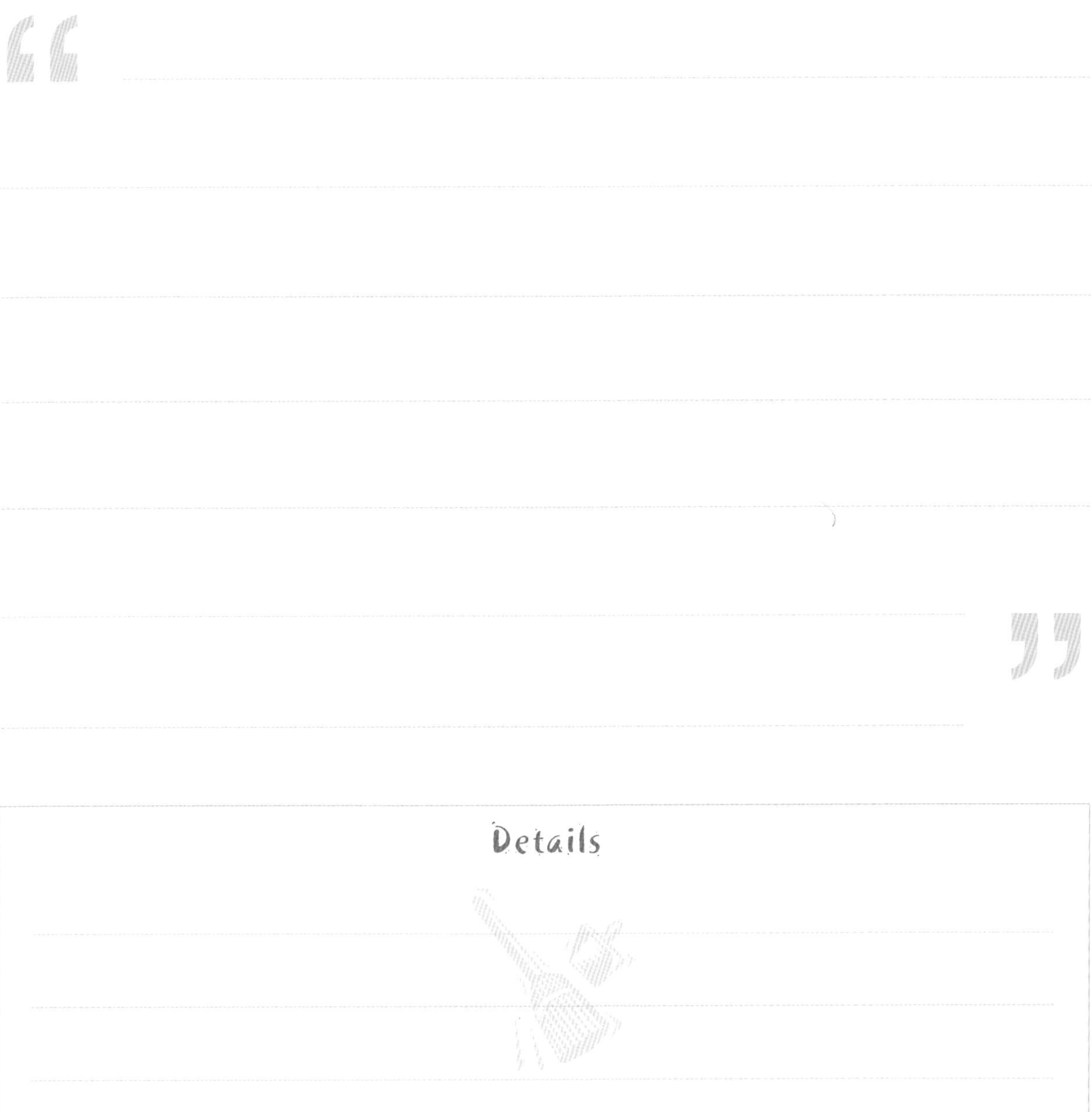

Details

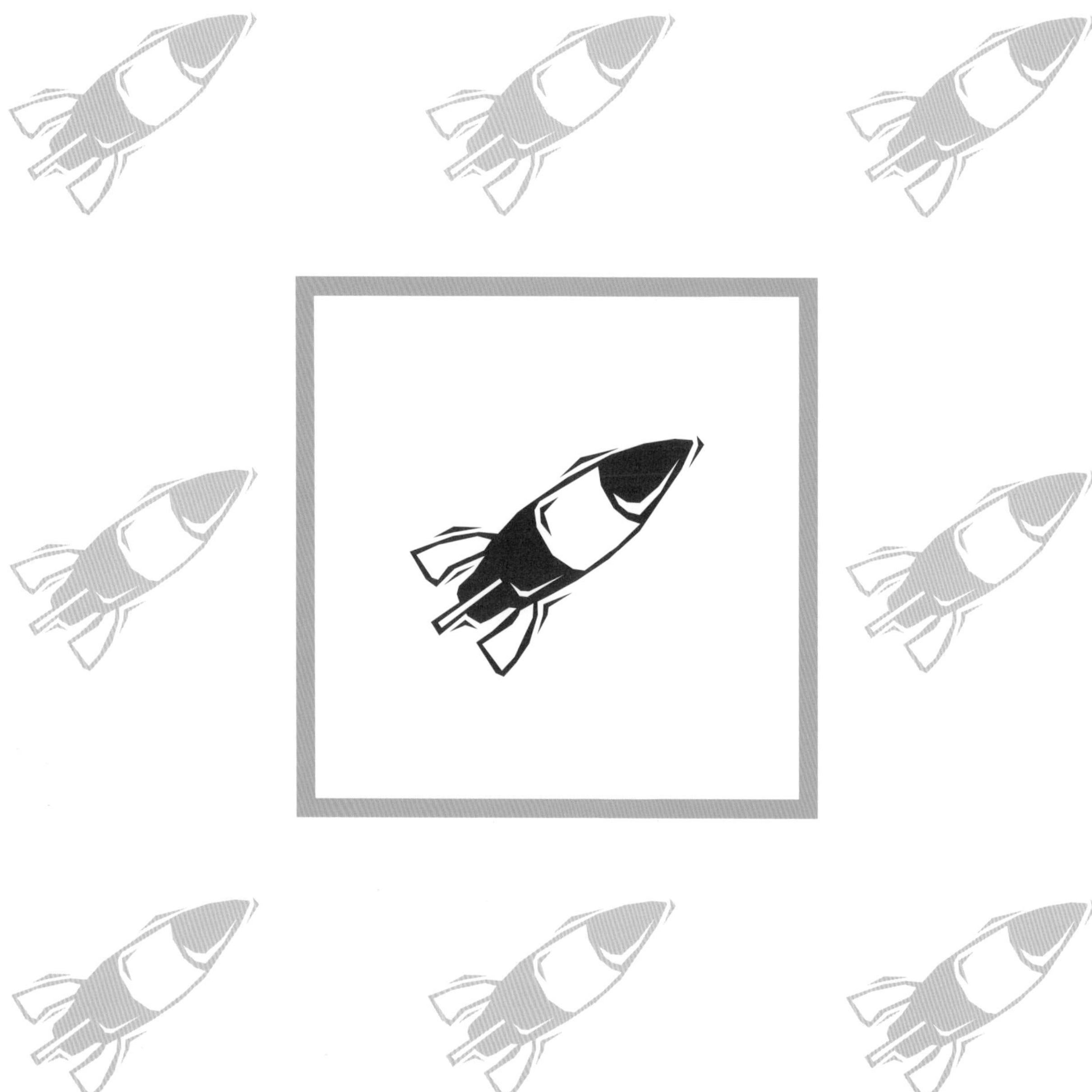

""

Details

Oh, What You Said!

“

”